Reading with Ricky
Ducks, Shells, and Swamps

Stories by Kathy Kranking
Illustrations by Christian Slade

Contents

2	Copycats
11	Learn More: Mallards
12	Slime Time
20	Learn More: Shell Dwellers
22	The Swamp Monster
30	Learn More: Animals of the Swamp

Copycats

Flora Skunk and Sammy Skunk were sitting at their picnic table drawing pictures. Sammy was peeking at his big sister Flora's paper to see what she was drawing. He liked to copy her.

Knowing that Sammy was watching her, Flora drew a circle. Sammy did the same. She drew a curve. So did Sammy.

Sammy kept copying. Then he noticed something about his drawing. "Hey—you drew me!" Sammy said. "I mean, I drew me."

"I saw you being a copycat," Flora said with a grin.

Ricky Raccoon and Bizzie Beaver walked up. "Hi, guys," said Ricky. "Can Bizzie and I draw pictures with you?"

"I have a better idea," said Sammy. "Let's play a copycat game."

"It looks like you're already playing that!" said Bizzie, looking down at the two pictures of Sammy.

RICKY ASKS

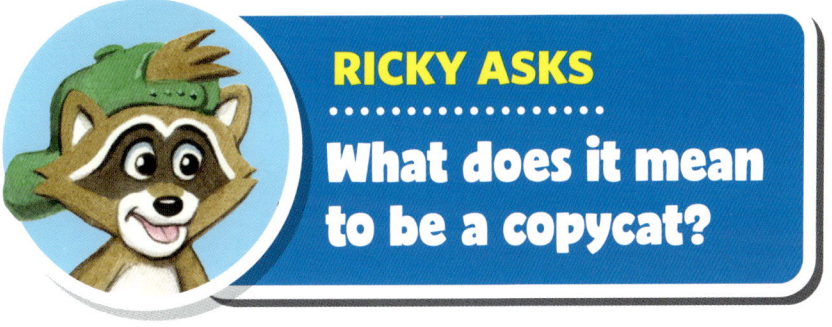

What does it mean to be a copycat?

"No, not with drawings," Sammy explained. "We can go for a walk and find animals to copy."

"I don't understand," said Flora.

"Don't worry, you will," said Sammy. "Just wait and see."

So the four friends headed off. Soon they saw a rabbit hopping. It stopped to look at them, wiggling its nose. Then it hopped away.

"Copy that rabbit!" said Sammy.

Ricky, Sammy, Bizzie, and Flora all began wiggling their noses and hopping. They hopped faster and faster. But then Flora hopped into Ricky, and Ricky fell into Bizzie, and Bizzie bumped into Sammy and they all landed in a giggling heap on the ground.

"Hopping is fun!" said Bizzie. "But I don't think this ever happens to rabbits!"

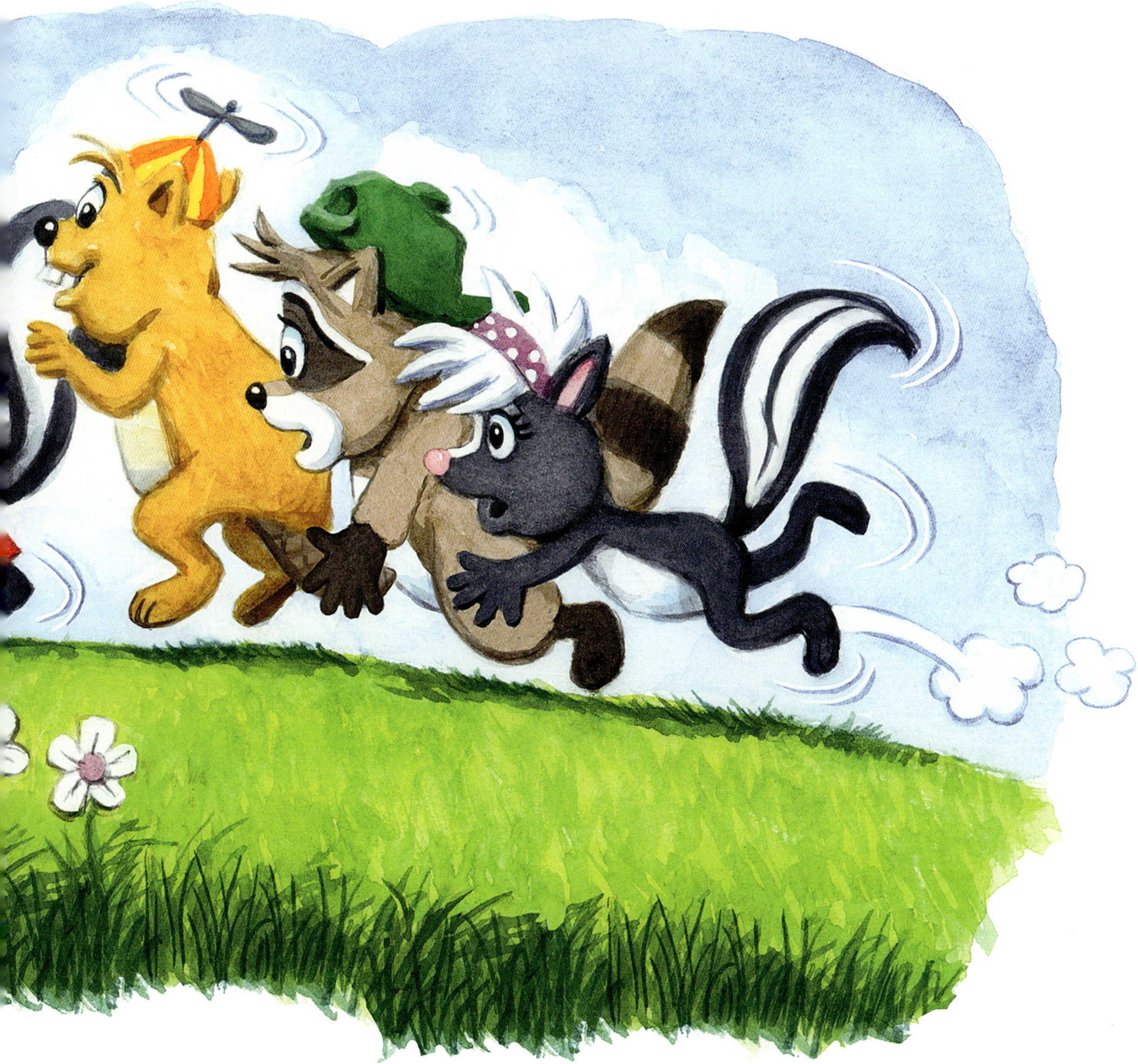

"OK," said Ricky, "let's go find another animal to copy."

The friends walked along until they came to Shady Pond. "Look!" said Flora. Floating gracefully on the water were two ducks.

"They're beautiful," said Ricky. As the friends watched, the two birds suddenly dipped their heads into the water, then flipped their rear ends up into the air.

Sammy giggled. "The ducks are doing headstands!" he said.

"That's how they reach underwater plants to eat," said Ricky.

"OK, copycats," said Bizzie. "Let's copy those ducks!"

The friends all crouched down and tried standing on their heads. Ricky got his legs up right away. So did Sammy. But Bizzie kept wobbling and toppling over. And Flora couldn't straighten her legs without losing her balance. Finally, all four of them were standing on their heads.

"You know," said Ricky, "the ducks are doing their headstands in the water." He brought his legs down and grinned at his friends.

"Ricky, you aren't serious, are you?" asked Flora.

FLORA WONDERS

Have you ever done a headstand?

Bizzie's eyes got big. "Headstands in the water?" he asked.

Ricky laughed. "Come on," he said, wading into the pond. "This will be the best copycat trick ever!"

The others followed him, laughing. "Don't forget to hold your breath!" Sammy said.

They all plunged their heads into the shallow water, trying to stand on their heads. And they did it! When they couldn't hold their breath any longer they came up, sputtering water and shaking it out of their ears.

"We make great ducks!" said Bizzie. "Hey, where'd they go?" he asked. The ducks had disappeared.

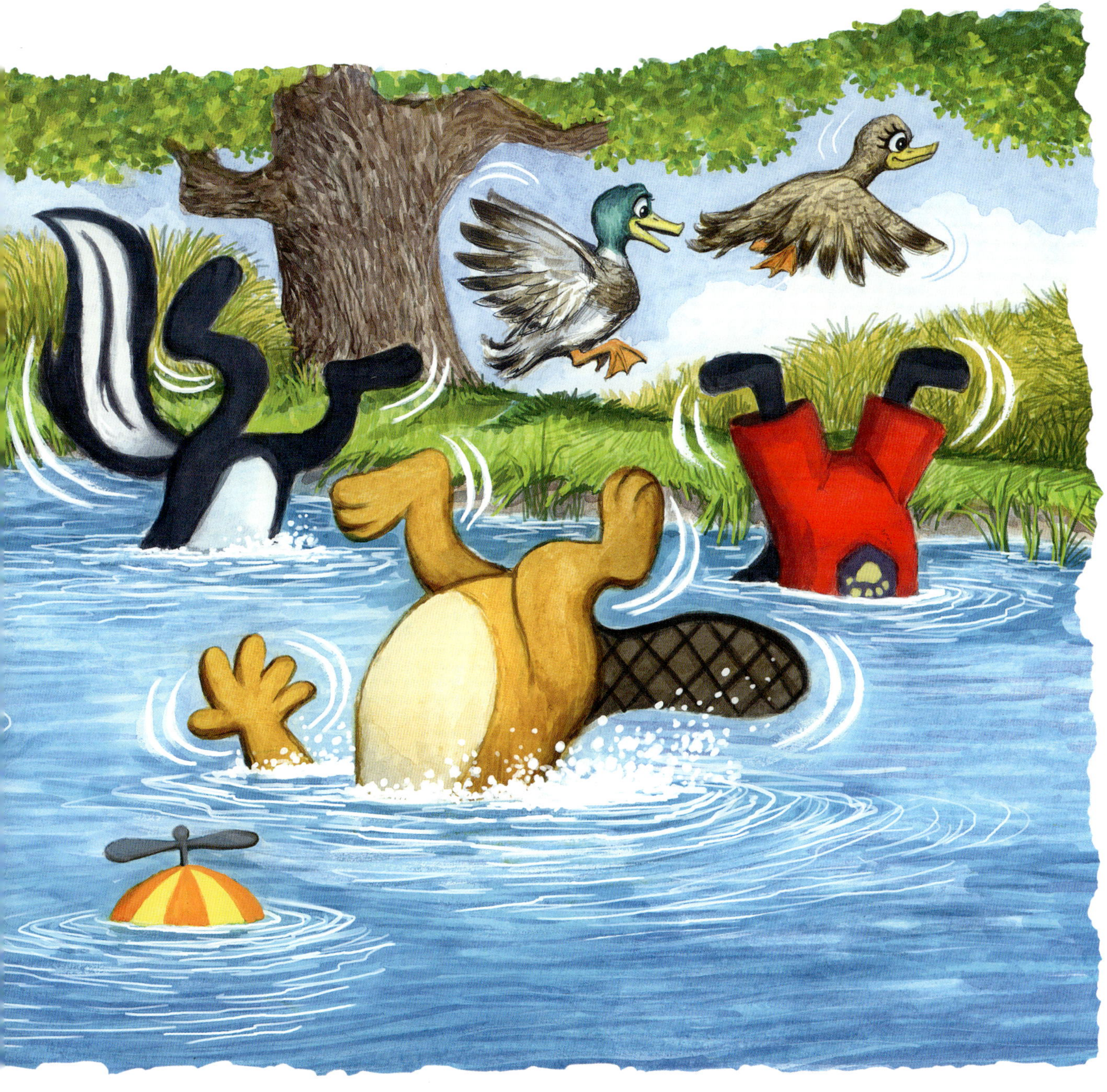

"I guess we scared them a little," Ricky said. "They must be along the shore behind those plants, where we can't see them."

Ricky and his friends waded back out of the water. Then Flora looked around. "Hey, where's Sammy?" she asked. The little skunk wasn't in the water. And he was nowhere in sight on the shore.

"That's strange," said Bizzie.

They all began calling for Sammy. And suddenly, there he was, jumping out from behind a tree.

"There you are, you sneak!" said Flora.

"I'm the very best copycat!" Sammy said happily.

"How do you figure that?" asked Ricky.

"Well," said Sammy, "the ducks disappeared—and so did I!"

BIZZIE WANTS TO KNOW

Why did Sammy hide behind the tree?

LEARN MORE

5 Things to Know About Mallards

1. Only male mallards have green heads. Females have mostly brown feathers.

2. Mallards are the most common duck in the world.

3. Male mallards do not quack.

4. Mallards turn bottoms up to find food in shallow water.

5. Baby mallards are called ducklings.

Slime Time

It was a cool evening. Ricky Raccoon and his pals were hanging out at the edge of the woods near Sunny Meadow.

"This rock is covered with shiny lines," said Flora Skunk.

"I know what that is," said Ricky. "It's dried slime!"

"Ew!" said Bizzie Beaver. "You mean like, someone sneezed on it?"

Ricky giggled. "No, silly. It's slime from snails. When snails crawl along, they leave slime trails."

Mitzi Mink crouched down to look more closely at the rock. "Wow! There sure are a lot of trails. It looks like a snail raceway!"

"That gives me an idea," said Bizzie. "Let's try to find some snails. Then we can have a snail race."

So the pals peeked under leaves, beneath rocks, and under logs. Soon Ricky, Flora, and Mitzi had each found a snail.

"Bizzie," called Ricky, "have you found your racer?"

RICKY WONDERS

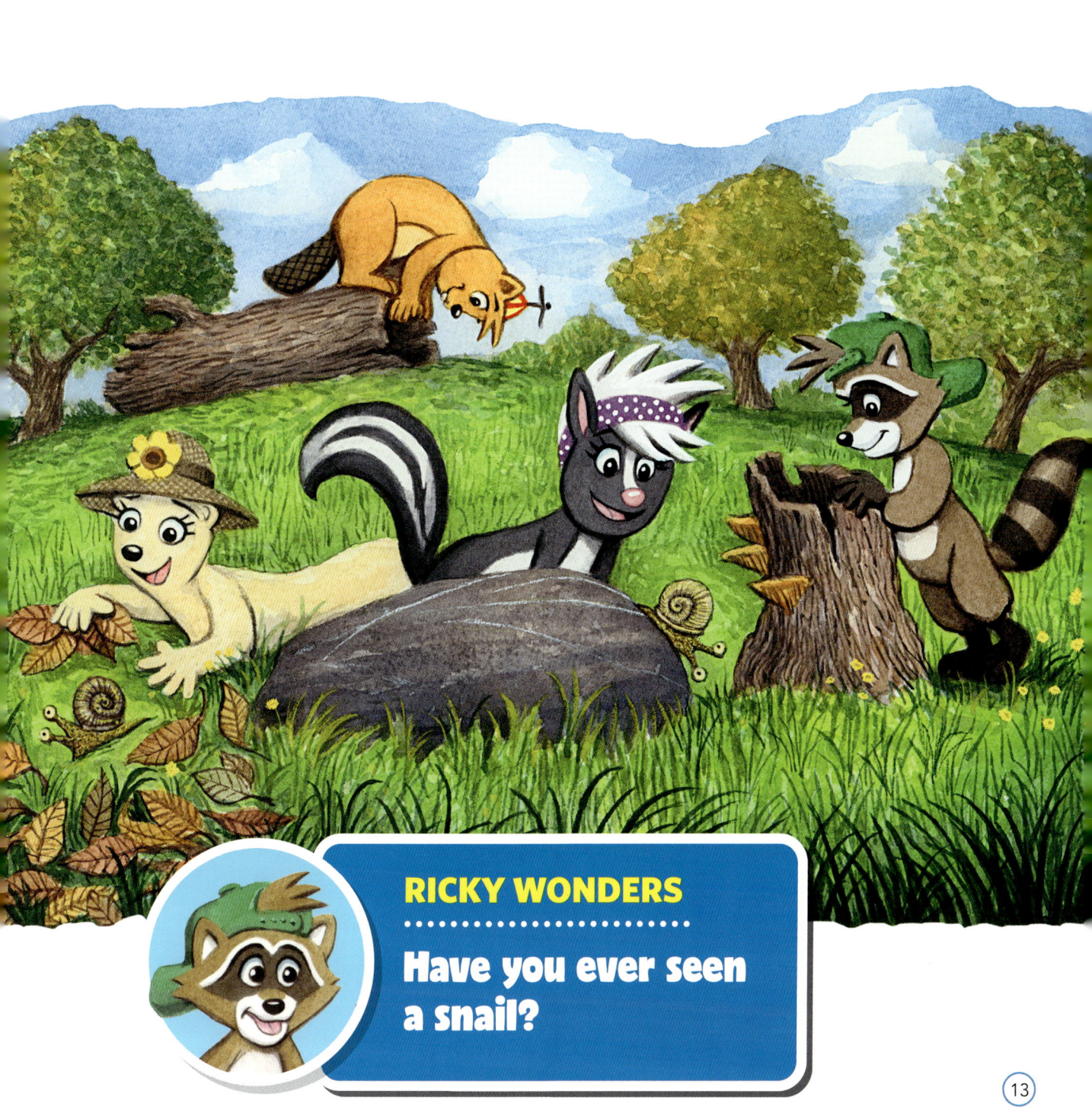

Have you ever seen a snail?

"Sure have," Bizzie said with a happy grin. He held out his paw. But he didn't have a snail. He was holding a tiny inchworm!

"This is Inchy," Bizzie said excitedly.

"Bizzie," said Flora, "you can't enter an inchworm in a snail race."

Bizzie's face fell. "Why not?"

"He's too fast," said Mitzi. "It wouldn't be fair."

"Well, I couldn't find a snail," said Bizzie. He thought a minute. "I know," he said. "What if Inchy gives the snails a head start?"

Ricky, Flora, and Mitzi decided that would be OK.

Flora watched her snail crawl across her paw. "I'm going to call my snail Speedy," she said. "Just look at her go! She's fast."

"Sorry," said Ricky, "but Lightning is going to slime circles around Speedy! Aren't you, Lightning?" he asked, as the snail climbed up his finger.

"Well, Rocket is going to blast past all of you!" said Mitzi.

"Let's use the rock as our racetrack," said Ricky.

The friends put a stick near the edge of the rock for a starting line. Then they put a blade of grass down for the finish line.

"OK," Ricky said, "on your mark . . ."

"You can do it, Speedy," whispered Flora.

"Get set . . ." said Ricky.

"Go get 'em, Rocket!" said Mitzi.

"Go!" cried Ricky, and the friends all set their racers down on the rock. Bizzie put Inchy at the starting line, while the others put the snails a couple of inches ahead of him.

FLORA WANTS TO KNOW

Who do you think will win the race?

"The race is on!" called Flora. As the friends watched, Lightning slowly moved forward. Inchy started inching along, but then turned to the left.

"No, Inchy. That's the wrong way!" Bizzie moaned.

Speedy was gliding along next to Lightning. But Rocket had pulled inside her shell and wasn't moving at all.

"Rocket," groaned Mitzi, "what are you doing?" But Rocket remained stubbornly still.

Ricky laughed. "Looks like Rocket ran out of fuel," he said.

Meanwhile, Inchy had continued to inch along the wrong way and was crawling down the side of the rock.

"I guess Inchy didn't want to race with snails," said Bizzie.

Meanwhile, Lightning and Speedy had almost reached the blade of grass finish line. Suddenly Lightning turned and began to crawl along next to the finish line.

"No, Lightning, you have to go across the finish line!" said Ricky.

"And Speedy wins!" exclaimed Flora, as Speedy crawled slowly across the blade of grass. "She's the champ!"

Mitzi took the blade of grass and put it in front of Rocket's shell. "Aw, Rocket," she said. "You were supposed to be crawling to this!" As she spoke, Rocket poked her head out of her shell. After a second or two, she began to nibble on the blade of grass.

"Oh, I see," said Mitzi with a giggle. "Rocket didn't want to *cross* the finish line. She wanted to *eat* it!"

BIZZIE WANTS TO KNOW

Would you rather have a snail or an inchworm?

LEARN MORE

Shell Dwellers

All of these animals are at home in a shell.

A box turtle's shell has a top and bottom. As the turtle grows, the shell grows with it.

A snail carries its shell on its back as it glides along on one foot. As a snail grows, its shell grows bigger, too.

A hermit crab drags its shell behind it. When the crab grows too big, it finds a new shell to move into.

The Swamp Monster

Sammy Skunk was sitting against a tree trunk reading a comic book called "Creature of the Swamp." Sammy was so wrapped up in the story that he didn't even notice when Ricky Raccoon, Flora Skunk, and Bizzie Beaver came walking up.

"There you are, Sammy!" said Flora.

The sound of Flora's voice took Sammy by surprise, and he screamed in fright. When he saw it was just his friends, he relaxed. "Oh, it's just you guys!" he said.

"Who did you think it was?" asked Ricky.

"Well, I was reading this story about a monster that lived in a swamp…." Sammy began.

"Oh, Sammy, you and your monster stories," said Flora.

"Don't you remember that we're taking a big hike today?" asked Ricky.

"We're all packed up and ready," said Flora. "So, let's go!"

"Oh, yeah," said Sammy as he stuffed his comic book into his pocket. Then they all headed off.

After the friends had been walking for a long time, Sammy said, "Hey, where are we hiking to, anyway?"

"We're going to a swamp," said Ricky.

"A swamp?" Sammy shouted. "Why would we go there? Don't you know that there are monsters in swamps?"

FLORA WANTS TO KNOW

What kind of books do you like to read?

"There aren't any monsters," said Flora.

"But in my comic book there was a scary monster," Sammy said.

"You'll see, Sammy," said Ricky. "A real swamp won't be anything like your comic."

But as the friends continued to walk, Sammy got more and more nervous. Finally, they came to the swamp—a place with lots of trees and the ground is covered with water. Built across the water was a wooden walkway.

"Cool! The swamp has a boardwalk!" said Bizzie. Then he took off running as he called out, "Last one there is a rotten egg!"

Ricky, Flora, and Sammy took off running after Bizzie. Once the four friends got to the boardwalk, they all stopped to look around.

The swamp was home to lots of animals. In just the first few minutes, they saw turtles, a rabbit, a woodpecker, and even a snake. Moss hung down from the limbs of the tall trees all around them.

25

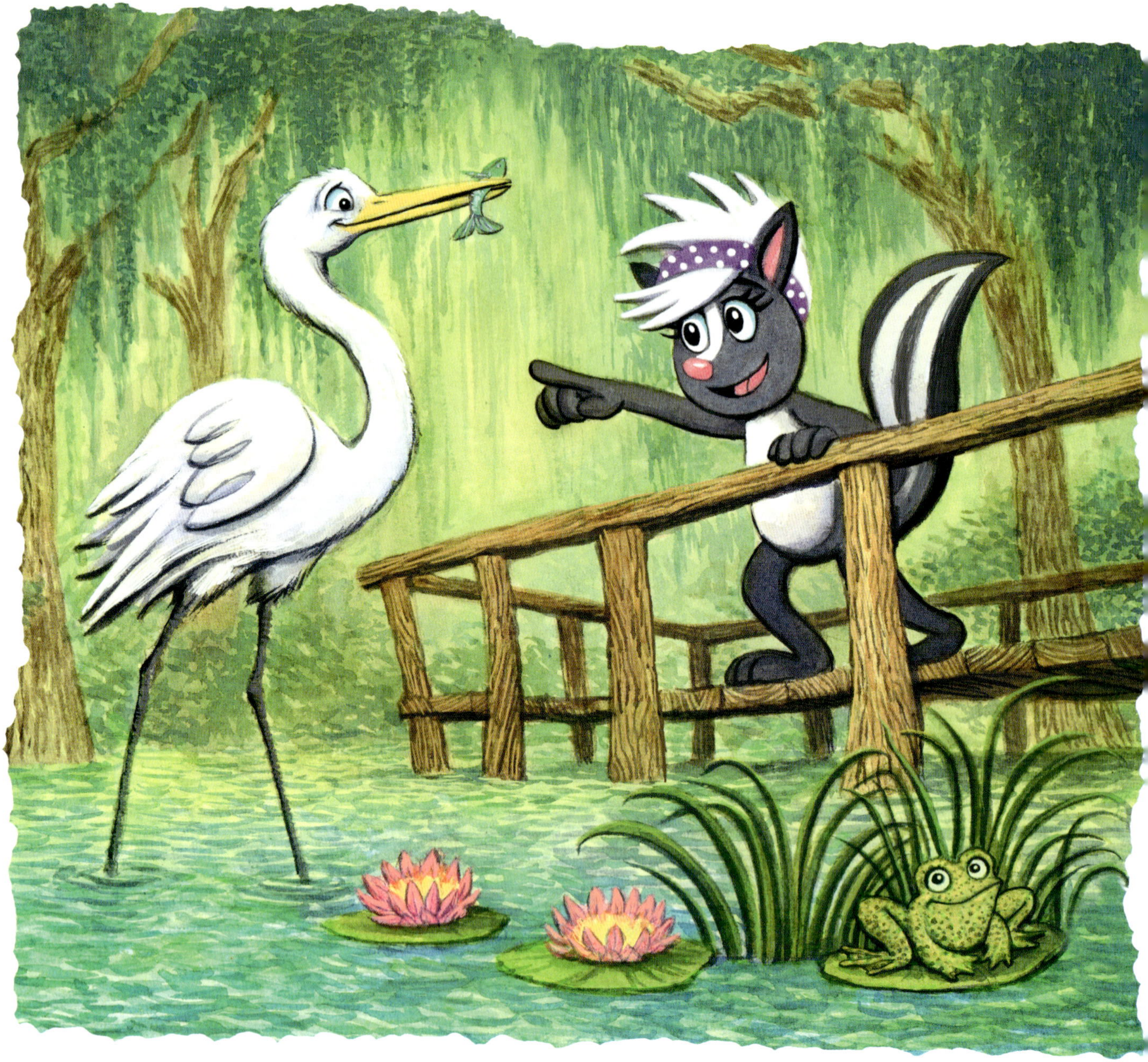

"Look!" said Flora. She pointed at a beautiful white bird standing in the shallow water. As the friends watched, the bird suddenly poked its long bill into the water and grabbed a fish. *Gulp!* In a second, the fish was gone.

The gang spent all afternoon exploring the swamp. Then it was time to head home. As they left the boardwalk, Flora asked, "What do you think of the swamp now, Sammy?"

"Well, I guess it's not really scary," Sammy said. "I haven't seen any monsters!"

"Nope," said Bizzie. He pointed up toward the branches of a tree. "None there," he said with a toothy grin.

Flora looked under a bush. "None here," she said.

"And none here, either," Sammy said with a smile, as he peeked around a tree trunk. Suddenly he gasped.

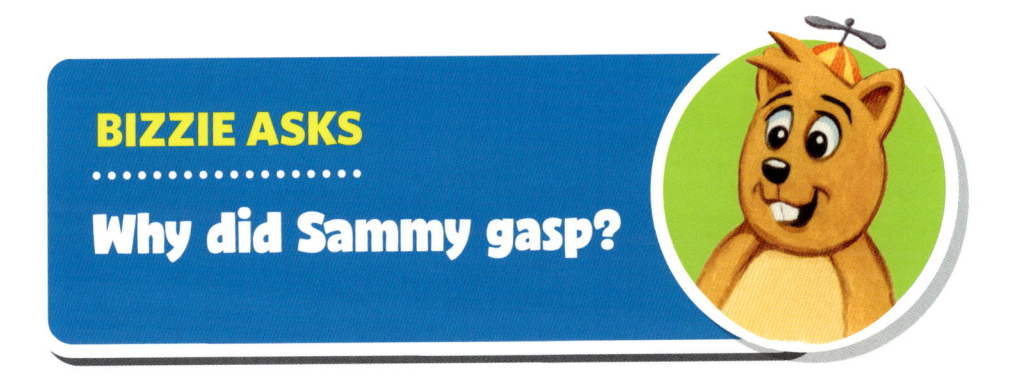

BIZZIE ASKS

Why did Sammy gasp?

Sammy was face to face with . . . a monster! It had scaly skin. It had long, sharp claws. And when it saw Sammy, it jumped straight up into the air!

"Yikes!" Sammy shouted. The others watched in surprise as the monster landed back on the ground. Then, in a split second, the monster ran off.

"What was that?" asked Bizzie.

Sammy was gasping. "A monster!" he said. "I told you!"

Ricky was smiling. "Relax, Sammy," he said. "That animal was not a monster."

Everyone looked at Ricky in surprise.

"I've seen pictures of that animal," Ricky said. "It's called an armadillo. Armadillos look like they're wearing suits of armor. And when they get scared, they jump straight up into the air."

Bizzie was grinning. "Hey, Sammy, you know what's funny?" he asked. "You were afraid of seeing a monster. But the 'monster' you saw was just as scared as you were!"

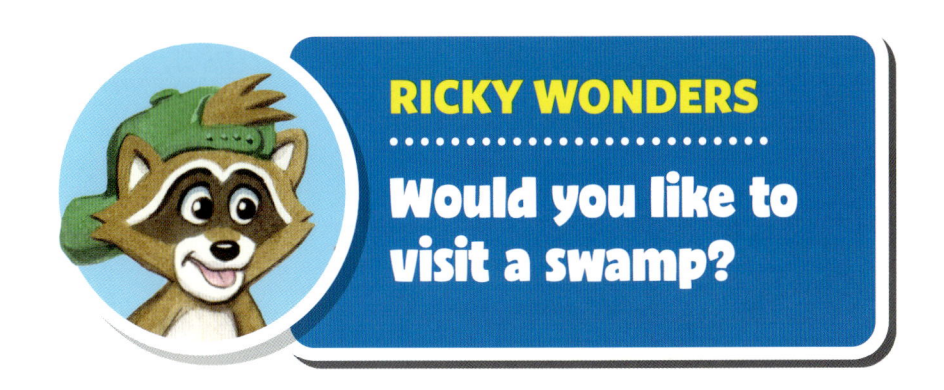

RICKY WONDERS

Would you like to visit a swamp?

LEARN MORE

Animals of the Swamp

A swamp is a woody area that is partly covered with water. Meet three animals that live there.

An **alligator** is at home on land and in muddy waters. It will eat almost anything.

Crayfish look like small lobsters. They live in the mud, so some people call them mudbugs.

An **anhinga** (an-HING-guh) catches fish in the water. Then it spreads out its wings to dry off.

Published by the National Wildlife Federation.

"Ricky and Pals" originally appeared in Ranger Rick Jr, a publication for children ages 4–7 in the Ranger Rick family of magazines.

Kathy Kranking, Author
Christian Slade, Illustrator
Molly Woods, Reading Consultant

Photo and Illustration Credits:
Page 11: Daniele Occhiato / Buiten-Beeld / Minden Pictures; Page 20: Lynn M. Stone / NPL / Minden Pictures; Page 21: Jean-Yves Grospas / Biosphoto / Minden Pictures (top), Wil Meinderts / Buiten-Beeld / Minden Pictures (bottom); Page 30: John Cancalosi / Biosphoto; Pages 30–31: Jack Desrocher (illustrations); Page 31: Modoki Masuda / Nature Production / Minden Pictures (top), James Christensen / Minden Pictures (bottom).

Copyright © 2021 by the National Wildlife Federation.

All rights reserved. No part of this book may be reproduced in any form or by electronic or mechanical means, including information storage and retrieval systems, without written permission from the publisher, except by a reviewer who may quote passages in a review.

Printed in the United States of America.

RangerRick.org

ISBN: 978-1-947254-28-2